D1545026

DISEASE-HUNTING SCIENTIST

Careers Hunting Deadly Diseases

EDWARD WILLETT

Enslow Publishers, Inc.
40 Industrial Road
Box 398
Berkeley Heights, NJ 07922
USA
http://www.enslow.com

Library of Congress Cataloging-in-Publication Data

Willett, Edward, 1959–
    Disease-hunting scientist : careers hunting deadly diseases / by Edward Willett.
       p. cm. — (Wild science careers)
    Includes bibliographical references and index.
    Summary: "Explores careers in and science of epidemiology through accounts of real-life
scientists"—Provided by publisher.
    ISBN-13: 978-0-7660-3052-7
    1. Epidemiology—Juvenile literature. I. Title.
    RA653.5.W55 2009
    614.4—dc22

                          2008004674

ISBN-10: 0-7660-3052-0

Printed in the United States of America

10 9 8 7 6 5 4 3 2 1

To Our Readers: We have done our best to make sure all Internet Addresses in this book were active and appropriate when we went to press. However, the author and the publisher have no control over and assume no liability for the material available on those Internet sites or on other Web sites they may link to. Any comments or suggestions can be sent by e-mail to comments@enslow.com or to the address on the back cover.

♻ Enslow Publishers, Inc., is committed to printing our books on recycled paper. The paper in every book contains 10% to 30% post-consumer waste (PCW). The cover board on the outside of each book contains 100% PCW. Our goal is to do our part to help young people and the environment too!

Photo Credits: AFP/Getty Images, pp. 16, 18; Associated Press, pp. 14, 100; CDC/Dr. Scott Smith, pp. 32, 36; CDC/Taronna Maines, p. 6; © Consortium for Conservation Medicine/Wildlife Trust, pp. 70, 74, 78, 79; Courtesy Jonathan Runstadler, pp. 57, 58, 63; © Edwin van Wier/iStockphoto.com, p. 47; James Cavallini/Photo Researchers, Inc., p. 68; M. Guerra, pp. 88, 92; Photo by Laurie Richardson, pp. 42, 43, 49; Public Health Agency of Canada, pp. 9, 29, 30; Science Source/Photo Researchers, Inc., pp. 8, 54, 86; Science VU/CDC/Visuals Unlimited, Inc., p. 23; Shutterstock, pp. 4–5, 38; Tek Image/Photo Researchers, Inc., p. 1.

Cover Photo: © Andreas Reh/iStockphoto.com

Contents

CHAPTER 1

Chasing Disease

Stringing mesh nets in Chinese caves to catch bats. Rolling along darkened African roads hoping to avoid armed rebels. Wearing a protective "space suit" to work in a high-tech lab. Scuba-diving on coral reefs off the coast of Florida. Camping in the Alaskan wilderness. . . .

You have to admit it all sounds pretty extreme. And those are just some of the things the scientists you will read about in this book have done while investigating diseases. You may have heard of some of these diseases, such as Ebola. Other diseases, such as black band disease, are probably new to you.

While some of the scientists in this book are medical doctors and others are biologists or veterinarians, almost all of them also call themselves epidemiologists. **Epidemiology** is the study of how often diseases affect different groups of people or animals, where different diseases develop, and why some people or animals develop them. Figuring out all these things is often very much like solving a mystery. That is why epidemiologists are often called "disease detectives."

More and more, the epidemiology of diseases in humans and the epidemiology of diseases in animals are linked. There is a good reason for this. According to one recent study, out of 1,415 **viruses**, **bacteria**, and parasites known to cause disease in humans, 61 percent are **zoonotic**. That means they can be transmitted between humans and animals. The same study indicates there are 175 disease-causing organisms that are considered "emerging," meaning the diseases they cause have only recently been identified. Of those new diseases, 75 percent are zoonotic.[1]

Some of the most dangerous new diseases began with animals. As people continue to move into areas

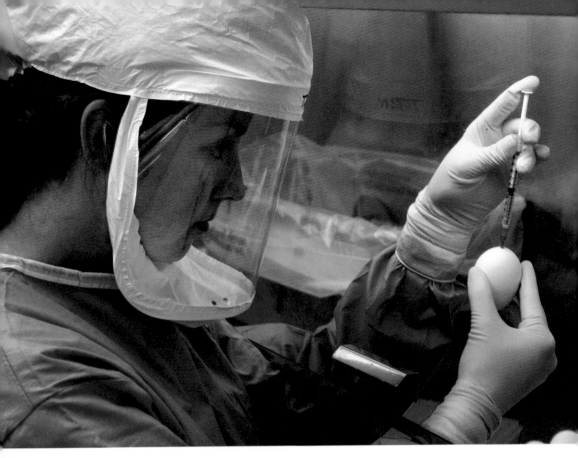

This scientist is using chicken eggs to study avian influenza, also known as bird flu. Avian influenza is a zoonotic disease that spread from birds to humans.

of the earth where humans have not lived before, they will continue to drive animals out of their natural habitats. Animals that have had very little contact with humans before will now have more and more. That means that there are likely to be more **emerging diseases** making the jump from animals to humans. And since international air travel is so common, those emerging diseases can quickly spread around the world.

To protect human health, we need to know more about how these organisms cause disease in humans, how they jump from animals to humans, and how outbreaks of these diseases can be controlled.

It is important to know how diseases affect our world. Disease detectives also work with nonhuman diseases, such as the black band disease that is killing coral reefs. Diseases like this can have a devastating impact on the environment as a whole, harming not only the species directly affected but all those that are linked to it within a particular habitat. Disease detectives, in other words, have their work cut out for them. As you will see in this book, they are up to the task. To learn what they can about emerging diseases and help those affected by them, they will go to any lengths, depths, and heights . . . no matter how extreme.

CHAPTER 2

Lisa Fernando: Marburg in Angola

"You've got to be kidding me!"

It was 2005. Lisa Fernando had just been told she would be flying to the African nation of Angola within a week. She was going to help battle an outbreak of Marburg hemorrhagic fever. Hemorrhagic fevers are particularly nasty diseases whose symptoms typically include a high fever and, worst of all, internal bleeding: victims can bleed to death inside their own skins.

Marburg hemorrhagic fever

Fernando had been working at the Canadian Science Centre for Human and Animal Health in Winnipeg, Manitoba, for two and a half years. She had started there shortly after she received her master's degree in medical **microbiology**—the study of microscopic bacteria and viruses that cause disease.

The Canadian Science Centre for Human and Animal Health is a joint facility, home to both the

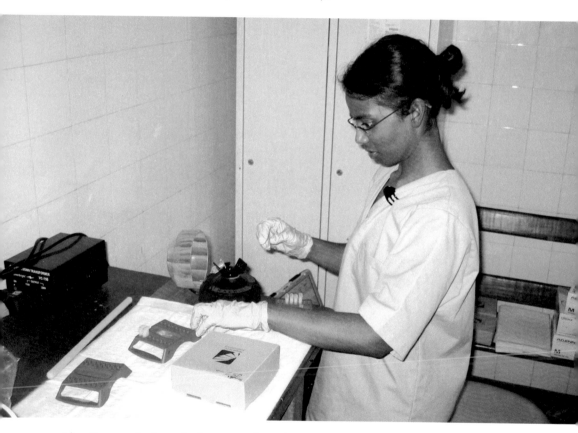

Lisa Fernando traveled to Angola, Africa, to help during an outbreak of Marburg hemorrhagic fever.

Public Health Agency of Canada's National Microbiology Laboratory and the Canadian Food Inspection Agency's National Centre for Foreign Animal Disease. It is also home to the country's only Level 4 laboratory. A Level 4 laboratory is one that can meet the strict safety standards for working with some of the world's most dangerous disease-causing agents, such as the Marburg virus.

Marburg is closely related to the Ebola virus, one of the best-known disease-causing agents that scientists study in Level 4 labs. But until the outbreak in Angola, confirmed by the World Health Organization in March 2005, nobody realized that Marburg could be just as deadly as Ebola.

There is no cure for Marburg hemorrhagic fever, just as there is no cure for Ebola. A person can easily become infected if he or she is in contact with bodily fluids, such as blood, from an infected person. At the time Fernando got the call to go to Angola, nine out of every ten people infected during the outbreak had died.

Well-prepared, but Still...

Even though the call to go to Angola had surprised her, Fernando was no stranger to working with deadly viruses. She had been training to do just that for her whole two and a half years at the Winnipeg lab. "Working with these viruses every day, I really had developed a comfort level," she said. "I felt well-prepared."

Still, when Dr. Heinz Feldmann, chief of special **pathogens** at the Public Health Agency of Canada—and Fernando's supervisor—told her she was going to Angola, her surprise was tinged with just a bit of fear. It would be her first overseas mission.

She battled the fear with logic, reminding herself, "We're not visiting the people in the field, and for the samples that we're handling, we're following all the same safety requirements as we do in Winnipeg." The only difference, she said, was that in the field they would not have "the fancy Level 4 lab."

Fernando knew she had been well trained, and she had a tremendous amount of trust in Dr. Feldmann. "He would never bring us into an area where he was worried about our safety or well-being," said Fernando, "I just had to trust in his experience."

Feldmann knew exactly what the team would be getting into, because he was already in Angola. He had gone there as part of the first team Canada sent, along with a mobile laboratory containing the equipment needed to diagnose Marburg. After three weeks in Angola, Feldmann found that the number of cases was increasing and the demand for the lab remained high. That was when he called for Fernando and medical officer Dr. Jim Strong to relieve him and his lab assistant.

"I didn't quite totally believe it until I was actually on the plane with Jim," Fernando said. In the week before they left for Angola, there had been too much planning and too many questions to concentrate on the reality of the situation. And, Fernando remembered, "With us being so far away, it was hard to really know what the situation was."

Do NOT Lean on the Airplane Door

The outbreak began in the northern Angolan city of Uige (pronounced WEEJ). Getting there was not easy. The scientists had to fly into Luanda, the capital of Angola, and then transfer to an hour-long flight on a tiny four-seat plane. "I remember the first flight out," Fernando said. "The pilot leaned over, pulled the door shut, and said, 'Just don't lean on it.' And I thought, 'This is the last flight I will ever take.' But at least it was adventurous!"

Conditions were primitive in Uige. The city and the surrounding countryside were badly affected by the civil war that had gripped Angola until just a couple of years before the outbreak. Fernando remembers the city being war-torn, with blown-out windows, gunshot holes, and dusty, deserted streets.

She and Dr. Strong were put up in a hotel . . . of sorts. They had to share one room, which they called the "honeymoon suite" because, unlike the other rooms, it had an attached bathroom. However, the bathroom did not have running water. "The shower was a bucket shower," Fernando said. "You had a big tub of water which they would cart in every second day at least, and then you would just bucket-shower that way." They used bottled water to brush their teeth. There was an air-conditioning unit, but no electricity to run it. The food was not always of the highest quality, either. Almost everyone on the expedition had diarrhea at some point.

Humble Surroundings, Important Work

The words "mobile laboratory" might make you imagine a gleaming air-conditioned semitrailer. The mobile lab Fernando and Strong worked in, however, was nothing of the sort. It had "no air-conditioning, no running water," Fernando said. Everything in it had been transported to Angola in six to eight rubber bins. The bins had simply been put aboard airplanes as checked luggage. Once the lab was delivered on-site, it could be up and operating within two hours.

The mobile lab contained various test kits; a

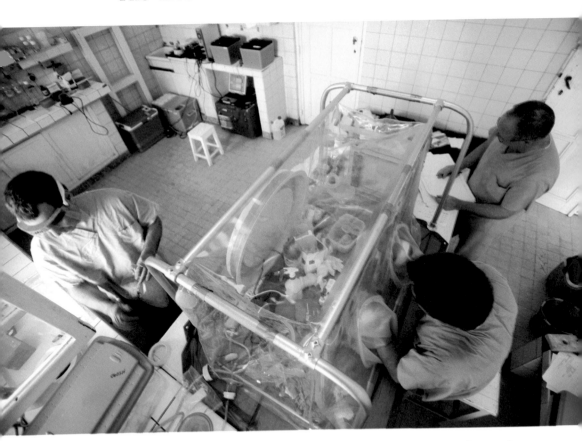

This is the mobile lab the Public Health Agency of Canada used during an outbreak of Ebola in the Democratic Republic of the Congo, Africa.

generator; a laptop computer designed to withstand humidity, dust, and heat; and a satellite phone. It also contained personal protection equipment to ensure the scientists did not infect themselves as they worked with samples from patients.

Using the lab, workers could determine who was infected and who was not. They did not want uninfected people to come into contact with infected people and catch the disease. They hoped to bring the outbreak under control by keeping the infected people away from the uninfected people.

The most important piece of equipment in the lab was a device called a real-time polymerase chain reaction (RT-PCR) unit. The RT-PCR could make many copies of the incredibly tiny bits of genetic material found inside viruses. It is hard to identify a virus if there is not enough of its genetic material to work with. Once there were enough copies, a virus could be identified.

Fernando and the others would receive samples—typically blood samples or swab samples—from people who might be infected with Marburg. They would examine those samples using RT-PCR to look for the presence of Marburg virus.

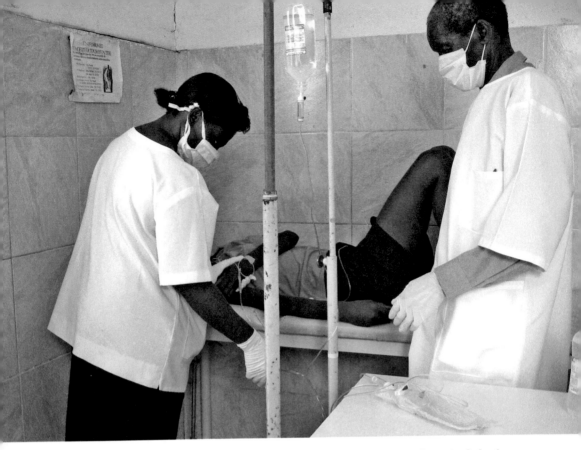

This woman was treated for Marburg in an Angolan hospital during the 2005 outbreak.

Taking Precautions

The lab was set up in a room at the Uige Provincial Hospital, where the outbreak was first identified. At the time of the outbreak, that hospital and its four doctors were the only healthcare available for the 1.5 million people in the region. Unfortunately, some of the earliest victims of outbreaks of diseases like Marburg and Ebola are often the medical staff at the hospitals where the first patients are taken. The

Angola outbreak was no exception. Among the first to die were two doctors and sixteen nurses.

Fernando says that by the time they got there, the doctors running the isolation ward would not even attempt to treat a patient until they had a diagnosis from the lab—because they feared being infected with the disease themselves. That made the Canadians' work doubly important. Fernando says that **malaria** is a huge problem in the region, and many of the children being brought to the hospital with symptoms similar to Marburg actually had malaria. Malaria can be treated, but the doctors refused to help the children until they were certain they did not have Marburg.

Fernando and Strong were not working directly with patients, but they still had to take precautions because they were dealing with samples that might contain Marburg virus. The lab tests themselves were run on killed virus—virus that could no longer cause disease.

While they were working with potentially live virus, Fernando and Strong wore something similar to the Level 4 "space suit" (described in more detail in chapter 3) they wore in the lab in Canada. The suit had its own battery-operated breathing supply, drawing in air

Despite the heat, these health workers are wearing protection suits to pick up a man infected with the Marburg virus in Uige, Angola.

through a HEPA (High Efficiency Particulate Air) fiter—a filter so fine even viruses cannot get through it. The suit also had rubber boots, taped at the top, and three pairs of gloves. "It's like wearing this big snowsuit and it gets very, very hot in there," Fernando says. "At times we were in that suit for an hour or two."

Ready to Go Again

After three weeks in the field, Fernando returned home for a month. Then she went back to Angola for another three weeks, because the World Health Organization wanted the lab to remain in Angola for three weeks after the last lab-confirmed case.

"We came home . . . the day before Canada Day

[July 1], and that was the best Canada Day ever. I remember thinking, 'Flushing toilets! Right on!' I had never been so grateful for running water and electricity!"

So far, Fernando has not been called for another outbreak. But she is ready to go if asked. "If there is the need, absolutely. I think that it is a great humanitarian effort."

Fernando's main work is focused on developing a vaccine for both Marburg and Ebola. She says that going to Angola really helped her to put her research into perspective. Seeing the effects of the disease in person has reinforced for her the importance of her job in Winnipeg.

High School Interest Pays Off

When she was growing up, working with deadly viruses was certainly not what Fernando thought she would end up doing as a career. "I had no idea what a Level 4 virus was," she says. Instead, the job just "fell into her lap," when Heinz Feldmann offered her a job as a biologist with the special pathogens group at the Canadian Science Centre for Human and Animal Health shortly after she completed working on her master's degree with him.

But if working with Level 4 viruses was not something she always thought she wanted to do, working in a research lab certainly was. Fernando says she became interested in biology and chemistry in high school and knew early on that she would study science in college.

"My second year I took a [microbiology] course, and I fell in love with bacteria. Then when I finished my degree I knew that I wanted to do research, so doing a master's was the first step in that direction."

She says that it was the best decision she ever made, because it helped her understand exactly what research involved. It also proved to her that she did not want to go on to obtain her PhD. With that more advanced degree, she says, "You kind of get stuck working behind a desk or writing grants or writing papers. I wanted to be more involved in the lab."

Even though she enjoys it, "Research is hard," Fernando says. "We often say in the lab it's 90 percent failure, 10 percent success."

Fernando says she laughs whenever she watches the 1995 movie *Outbreak*, perhaps the best-known fictional version of the kind of work she does. "I love the way they find a cure in 24 hours, and the scientists fall in love. Really, we don't lead glamorous lives like

LISA FERNANDO'S
CAREER ADVICE

Lisa Fernando's advice to young people interested in a career like hers is simple and straightforward: "Take all your science courses." Even though she didn't plan on pursuing physics, she says, she still took physics courses.

"Ask lots of questions, and find out about research opportunities," Fernando advises. "During my undergrad degree at the University of Winnipeg, I pursued the honors program which required you to complete a research project and write a thesis. The project I chose was not necessarily in my interest area; we were studying **algae**!"

Even unrelated research can prove to be a valuable experience: "Although it was completely irrelevant to what I'm doing now, just the process of doing research, understanding that things do not always work out, and realizing the type of traits you need as a researcher— that experience was very helpful."

As a result, she suggests anyone interested in becoming a research scientist try to pursue some type of research at college, "whether it be a summer job or a thesis course."

that. Research is hard: it's mostly failure. You get maybe one day of success out of the whole year. You have to be the type of person who can put up with that frustration and be very patient."

A Hero? No Way!

Fernando says the question she was most often asked by media in Canada at the time of the outbreak was, "Do you consider yourself a hero?"

She found it hard to believe anyone would even ask her that question. "Everyone I know in this business, the colleagues of mine that went to Angola, none of us are in this for the glory or the money, because there isn't a lot of money in science," Fernando says. "We're not in this for the front-page news, not at all.

"We're just here to do our job."

CHAPTER 3

James Strong: Working in Level 4

It is a staple of movies and TV shows: the Level 4 lab, where scientists in "space suits" race against the clock to find a cure for the mysterious disease that is killing people in the outside world. In the movies, scientists are glamorous, handsome, beautiful—and manage to fall in love, despite the space suits, and perform amazing feats of research

Ebola virus

WHAT ARE CONTAINMENT

Containment levels describe the measures a laboratory uses to prevent the accidental escape of the disease-causing bacteria or viruses scientists are researching there.

In a Level 1 lab, scientists work with microorganisms that do not cause disease in healthy adults. Two examples are E. coli (a kind of bacteria that can cause food poisoning, but isn't contagious) and infectious canine hepatitis virus, which makes dogs sick, but not humans.[1] The only necessary protective measure is a sink for washing hands.

A Level 2 lab is used for research on disease-causing microorganisms that can be worked with safely in the open, provided there is no risk of splashing or spraying. Closed cabinets, splash shields, face protection, gowns, and gloves are used as needed. Examples of Level 2 microorganisms are those that cause measles, salmonella, and Hepatitis B.

Level 3 labs are where researchers work with microorganisms that can cause serious, potentially deadly

just in time for a happy ending as the credits roll. But what is it like to work in a Level 4 laboratory in real life?

Dr. James Strong knows. As was mentioned in the last chapter, he accompanied Lisa Fernando to Angola. However, Strong spends more time in the National Microbiology Laboratory (the Level 4 laboratory in Winnipeg, Canada) than he does traveling to outbreaks. In fact, as head of the Cell Biology

LEVELS?

infections, and can be transmitted through breathing. In Level 3 labs all samples are handled inside closed, airtight cabinets. The lab itself usually has controlled access and the air going into and out of it is carefully filtered. Examples of Level 3 microorganisms are those that cause tuberculosis (an infectious disease that primarily attacks the lungs) and some forms of encephalitis (inflammation of the brain).

Finally, Level 4 labs are designed to enable researchers to work safely with dangerous and exotic samples that cause life-threatening diseases that can potentially be transmitted through the air, and for which no vaccine or effective treatment exists. The lab has its own ventilation system and nothing goes out of it—no air, and no waste materials—without being thoroughly decontaminated. Workers in Level 4 labs all wear "space suits" for which air comes from outside the lab. Examples of Level 4 microorganisms are the viruses that cause the Ebola and Marburg hemorrhagic fevers.[2]

section of the Department of Special Pathogens, he spends at least a couple of hours in the lab on most working days.

So how did Dr. Strong end up working in a lab that requires such extraordinary safety measures?

Although he is a pediatrician (a medical doctor specializing in children) by training, Strong says he has also done work in **virology**, the study of viruses. While training to be a pediatrician, Strong was looking for a research focus when one of the infectious disease doctors suggested he speak to Heinz Feldmann, the chief of special pathogens at the National Microbiology Laboratory. "He said, 'Would you be interested in working on some of these more nasty pathogens like Ebola and Marburg?' and I thought, 'Yes!'" Strong recalls.

Dr. Strong had always been interested in virology, an interest sparked in part by the outbreak of Ebola in Kikwit, Zaire (pronounced "zah-eer"), now known as the Democratic Republic of the Congo. The outbreak occurred in 1995, during Strong's medical training, and he was soon working with Feldmann to create a research program they could work on together.

Where Is Ebola Hiding?

Dr. Strong's research is focused on how the Ebola virus is transmitted from animals to humans.

"One of the big 'holy grails' as far as Ebola and Marburg research is [concerned is] what the reservoir is," he says. A "reservoir," or "**reservoir species**," is a species of animal in which the virus may circulate constantly without much effect. It does not cause serious illness until it jumps from the reservoir species to another species—such as humans—that is not adapted to it.

"There's been a lot of suggestion that [the Ebola virus] is in fruit bat species right now, but no one has ever been able to prove that in the field. We think that in the case of most of these Ebola outbreaks, a non-human primate—a monkey or a great ape—has been involved somewhere in the transmission to the human outbreak. What we don't know is how the primate is getting it."

Those species suffer from Ebola even more than humans—their fatality rates are even higher—which makes it unlikely they are the reservoir species, Dr. Strong says. "They'd be killed off as quickly as we would. We would be a lousy reservoir species as well!"

Some of Dr. Strong's past research suggested that mice or other small rodents might be involved in transmitting the disease. His current research examines some of the ways in which the Ebola virus could potentially be transmitted from rodents or bats to primates.

How much time Dr. Strong spends in the Level 4 lab depends on what he is doing, but since a lot of his research is carried out on cell cultures and infected cells, he is in the lab most days—including weekends, during an experiment—but usually not for much longer than two or three hours at a time. Occasionally, however, an experiment will require him or other researchers to be in the lab several times during the day and through the night.

Entering Level 4

The process of entering the Level 4 lab starts long before Dr. Strong dons the space suit, with much of the prep work occurring in the Level 2 (see sidebar on page 24–25) area. That work includes culturing—growing—the cells that will be infected with the virus inside the lab and gathering any necessary supplies that have to be taken into the Level 4 lab.

With supplies ready and everyone notified about his upcoming entry into Level 4, Dr. Strong is finally ready to go in.

The first step is to "strip down to what you're born with," Dr. Strong says. After that, the researchers put on surgical scrubs before entering through a big set of double doors, only opened by a large hand crank. Once inside the room, a protective suit is donned.

The suits are constantly checked to ensure they are secure. Each time one is used, the researcher carefully inspects it visually. Once a week, the suits are filled

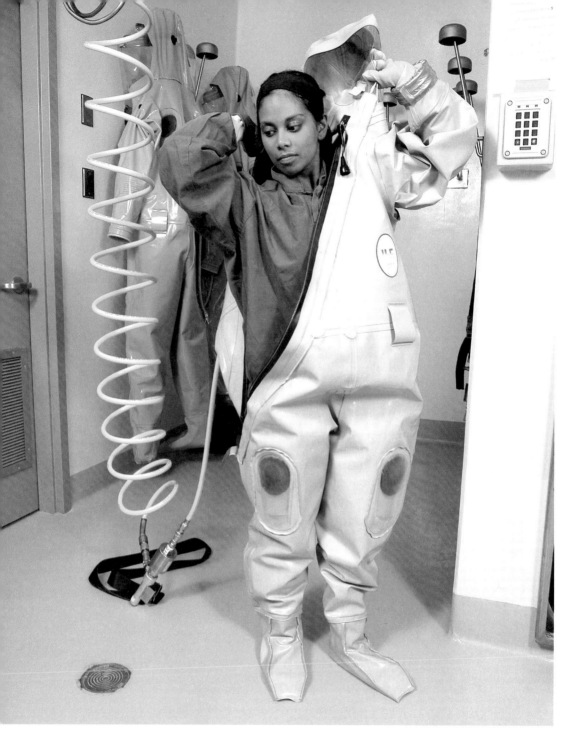

The Level 4 suit goes on over a pair of surgical scrubs. An air hose is attached on the back to give the researcher clean air to breathe.

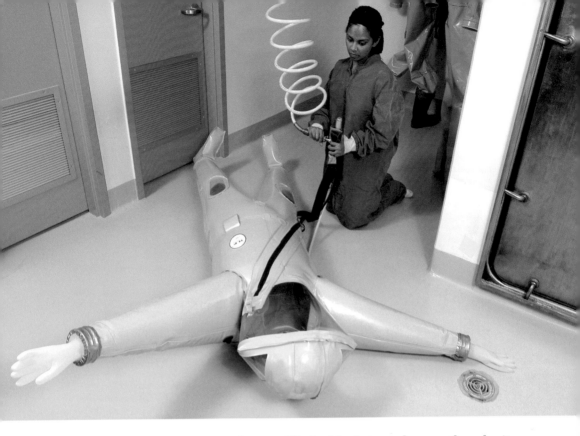

Each week, the "space suits" are filled with air to make sure they don't have any holes in them. Even a tiny hole could let a virus in and be potentially dangerous for a researcher.

with air and examined to make certain they have not sprung any leaks.

After examining the suit, the researcher puts it on and makes sure it is sealed. Outside, every researcher has a "backup buddy," a person with whom a researcher in the lab can stay in constant contact, usually by radio. That way, if a problem occurs, someone outside the lab is immediately aware of it. Researchers tell their backup buddies how long they plan to be in the lab, and what they will be doing inside.

After passing through another set of double doors with a chemical shower between them, the researcher has entered the Level 4 suites. The chemical shower automatically activates as soon as the researcher has passed through, decontaminating the room between the doors which has just been opened to the Level 4 area.

Finally, in Dr. Strong's words, "you call out to your radio buddy: 'I am going to Level 4.'"

Working in Level 4

Inside the lab itself, the work that is carried out is not very different from similar work on less-dangerous germs. The deadly viruses themselves, however, are stored in liquid nitrogen, which keeps them frozen and inactive. Their removal from storage is tightly controlled. The researchers must tell others ahead of time that they are removing a virus sample and note the exact quantities being taken out. They also must let others know what the sample of the virus is to be used for and how they plan to dispose of it.

All of that is to ensure nothing potentially infectious is left somewhere where it might pose a risk to researchers or could possibly be carried out of the lab.

Although the researchers wear triple gloves and "space suits" in the Level 4 lab, they are still able to move around freely.

The Level 4 "space suits" are easier to move around in than one might think. As Dr. Strong says: "Most people find them quite comfortable, unless they just do not like enclosed spaces."

Each researcher tends to wear the same suit every time he or she goes in, although frequent users often share a suit with researchers who only go in once in a while. The researchers wear triple gloves—two thinner inner gloves and a thicker outer one—which cut down on sensation, but this is no different from what a surgeon would wear to perform some types of surgery. Nevertheless, it takes much longer to perform any task in Level 4 than it would in an ordinary Level 2 lab, especially when you figure in the time needed just to get in and out.

"If it was going to take you fifteen minutes on the outside, it would take you more like an hour or an hour-and-a-half on the inside with all the preparation work," Dr. Strong says.

"It's Quite Peaceful"

Despite the inconvenience of getting in and out, Dr. Strong enjoys working in the Level 4 lab. "It is quite peaceful. You have the nice white background, a gentle breeze on your face, and a little bit of white noise. And you don't have pagers and cell phones and other things going off in there."

That is important, because even with all the precautions, "You want to stay focused," Dr. Strong says. "You are not often being tapped on the shoulder and being asked, 'Excuse me, would you pass the pipettes?' or something like that. You get a heightened sense of both personal space and focus."

There are never very many people working in Level 4 at the same time. Regulations allow for up to ten people between the National Microbiology Laboratory's Level 4 lab and the Canadian Food Inspection Agency's Level 4 lab, housed in the same building. However, two to six is more typical, with six being much less common than two.

Even though everything possible is done to make the Level 4 lab safe to work in, Dr. Strong says he never forgets he is working with deadly viruses. "I think it is always in your head." Dr. Strong always stays alert to possible risks: "In a Level 2 lab, if you were to knock something off [the work bench], you might end up reaching quickly to grab for it. In Level 4 you are much more cautious about it. You don't make any quick movements."

The biggest risk is puncturing both the suit and

your skin. A small hole in the suit is not particularly dangerous, because the air inside it is at a higher pressure than the air in the lab, meaning that lab air cannot get in through a small puncture. And the lab air itself is completely renewed every three minutes by a special ventilation system.

"You occasionally do get a hole in the glove," Dr. Strong says, "which means that you have to quickly dunk your hand into some disinfectant and take yourself out of that environment."

Even when the researchers are working with the viruses, he notes, the work is done inside a **biosafety** hood or cabinet. "Certainly the risk of exposure is very, very low, even with a punctured suit."

Getting Out

When the time comes to leave, all the materials used in the experiment are carefully secured and put away. Then it is time for decontamination.

The researchers dunk their hands in disinfectant to kill any microorganisms that might have somehow managed to attach themselves, then exit into the chemical shower, located between the set of double doors. Still wearing the suit, they take a five-minute shower: two minutes of MicroChem (a disinfectant

Before entering or leaving the Level 4 labs, a researcher has to go through a chemical shower. This helps make sure no outside elements can interfere with the Level 4 research, and also that no potentially dangerous disease specimens are carried outside the lab.

chemical) and three minutes of water to rinse off the MicroChem, scrubbing at the same time to clean off anything sticky that might be on the suit. Dr. Strong says researchers also rinse off their air hoses to make sure nothing got in when the hoses were hooked up or disconnected.

No more than two people can be in the chemical shower at the same time. Once the shower is over, the researchers go through the second door into the suit-change area. They take off their suits, then peel off their surgical scrubs and take a personal shower at least three minutes long. After that, they put on their regular clothes and exit the lab.

"A Fairly Untapped Area"

Dr. Strong enjoys his research in what he calls "a fairly untapped area."

"A lot of [research subjects] that you can apply to other viruses have not been studied [with the Level 4 viruses] because of the nature of the organisms and the nature of the level of containment that you need. So anything you can shed light on is brand new. I think that is probably the best thing about it."

He does not consider himself a daredevil for working in a Level 4 lab. "When I got into it originally I thought, 'Wow, that would be so cool to try to do this stuff in a Level 4 lab and be involved in outbreaks and things like that.' But now," he says, "it is pretty much the same as you would do in a normal Level 2 lab; you just have to have the added time and pain-in-the-butt factor of putting on a suit, chemical showers—that sort of thing."

He admits, though, that when he tells people outside the lab what he does for a living, they are sometimes reluctant to shake his hand.

"People always ask, 'Did you wash your hands today?'" he laughs. "But sometimes if I've gone into Level 4 I am cleaner than anybody, because I have had six personal showers by the time I am done with my day!"

CHAPTER 4

Laurie Richardson: What's Killing the Coral?

Dr. Laurie Richardson grew up on and in the water—not surprising, since her father was in the Navy. Even so, she never thought that her chosen field of scientific study, microbiology, would lead her into the oceans . . . until, one day, it did.

Today, Richardson is a professor of biology at Florida International University in Miami. Her research into black band disease in coral reefs means that she spends a lot of each summer in the water, sometimes scuba diving for several hours a day.

There are 110,900 square miles of coral reefs in the world's oceans. That sounds like a lot, but it is less than one tenth of one percent of the total area of the ocean floor. But despite their small size, coral reefs play an important role in the health of the ocean, because they support more than a million species of marine life. They are also important to the humans who live near the oceans. Coral reefs and the organisms that live on and around them provide food for many tropical islanders and attract tourists.

However, coral reefs are dying from pollution, overfishing, and a variety of diseases—including Dr. Richardson's focus, black band disease. In fact, scientists predict that if nothing changes, 40 percent of the world's coral reefs could be dead by 2010.[1]

A Long Way From the Water

Despite having grown up near the water, Dr. Richardson started college just about as far away from the ocean as possible—in Boulder, Colorado. She majored in fine arts, chemistry, and environmental biology, then went on to get her PhD in microbiology.

Her focus in her PhD research was "**microbial mats**," communities of microbes that live in the sulfur-rich water that flows out of hot springs. From there she went to Wisconsin where she worked on a NASA research project with scientists who were using data from satellites to study aquatic ecosystems. They needed someone like Dr. Richardson who was knowledgeable about bacteria that are photosynthetic—bacteria that, like plants, can make their own food when exposed to sunlight.

She eventually arrived in Florida with a NASA-funded grant to work on algal pigments (the compounds that give algae their color) and remote sensing—not knowing that her work in hot springs and bacteria would both come into play.

One day, just for fun, she went scuba diving on a coral reef, and somebody asked her what she thought about the algae killing the corals. "They showed me black band disease on the reef," Dr. Richardson explains. "I took one look at it and could see immediately that it was exactly like the kind of microbial communities that are found in hot spring outflows. And then I looked in the literature, and nobody had done anything at all with these communities. And that was how my whole research started."

That kind of "aha!" moment, that sudden grasp of a previously unknown connection, is what makes science exciting, Richardson says. "These days they call that interdisciplinary science. Somebody from another discipline [field of science] comes and looks at a problem and says, 'Hey! That's obvious! Look at what is going on!'"

Underwater Fieldwork

Most of Richardson's day-to-day time is spent teaching, writing papers and proposals, or working in her laboratory, but she also spends a good deal of time out in the ocean with graduate students, undergraduate students, and research collaborators. Together they collect samples and monitor the progress of disease on the reef. Most of that work takes place during "disease season," which is summertime in the Florida Keys and off the islands of the Bahamas.

Richardson assembles a team for each "mission," during which they dive every day for ten days—she refers to that time as the "intense field work." After

Dr. Laurie Richardson is a microbiologist and biology professor who studies black band disease in coral.

that, they return to the lab and work with samples they have collected.

On a typical mission day, the team prepares all of their pieces of equipment: sterile sampling syringes, sterile vials for samples, plastic and mesh bags, diving equipment, underwater slates, and coolers, to name a few. The research boat leaves the dock at about eight in the morning. The team also comes prepared to work safely: "Once we are on the reef we always have a very specific field plan of who is diving with who, and what samples we are going to get."

Coral samples are taken with numbered, sterilized syringes. "When you are underwater, you just reach your hand into your bag and grab one syringe by random, take your sample, and then record very carefully on your slate the number on the syringe and what that sample is, and a description of the diseased coral."

The day's work isn't done when they return to shore. From processing samples to transcribing all of the data collected that day into a computer file or

Richardson and her team do their fieldwork underwater—taking samples, measurements, and descriptions of coral. They use their findings to monitor disease on the coral.

field notebook, there are sometimes several hours of work before a day are truly complete. It makes for a long, hard day, Richardson says. "But it's fun, too!"

At least, most of the time.

Not Always Fun

One risk of diving is decompression sickness, also known as "the bends." While a diver is underwater his or her body is compressed by the weight of the water above. Gases can dissolve in the bloodstream under pressure. When the diver surfaces, the gases expand, forming bubbles in the bloodstream that can cause extreme pain. They can even be life-threatening.

Richards recalled one mission where she got the bends while exploring a reef along what they call a "transect line"—this is simply a straight line marked across an area where scientists are taking samples. The researchers follow the line and take samples at regular intervals.

"It took an hour," Richardson explains, "going down along this transect and counting the number of diseased corals and then coming back, very slow and very gradual."

Over the next two dives they did a disease survey, counting corals and taking note of which species were present and which were diseased. To do that, one diver swam in circles with a line tethered to a fixed point at the circle's center. While that diver counted diseased and healthy corals, the second diver made sure the line didn't get caught on anything.

Keeping an eye on that line was Dr. Richardson's job. This meant she wasn't doing much actual swimming while being in the freezing cold water. On her last dive (of only eight feet) Richardson was performing some heavy work with an underwater drill, trying to loosen some black band–infected coral for sampling. Going from the calm of monitoring a line to using a heavy drill in the freezing water, Dr. Richardson ended up getting decompression sickness—the bends.

To treat the bends, Richardson says, "They put you in a pressurized chamber and increase the pressure in there comparable to the depth of 60 feet of water. You are breathing pure oxygen."

While she was well within the safety guidelines to prevent decompression sickness, it is "just something that can happen when you are out there working and you dive hundreds and thousands of times," Richardson says.

A Scary Moment

Something even scarier happened on another dive, when Richardson's research team was working in the Bahamas near Bemini, off of a fairly large, anchored research boat.

A strong surge—what they call a powerful underwater current—came up, pulling sediment from the ocean floor, which ruined the team's visibility. Richardson and the two graduate students with her had to grab metal bars planted in the ocean floor and pull themselves blindly in the direction where they thought the anchor was.

"Fortunately we found the anchor, because if we had got caught in that current and got away from the boat we would have been off in the Gulf Stream [current] and who knows where. . . ."

The coral itself poses some risk to divers as well. Corals are living animals, with an extremely thin layer of living tissue (often less than a millimeter—one twenty-fifth of an inch—thick) over a rocklike skeleton of calcium carbonate. "If you grab onto them or get knocked into them or if your buoyancy control is bad and you crash into them . . . and break that tissue then that is really sharp rock. You're going to get cut," Dr. Richardson warns.

Corals may look like plants, but they are actually living animals. Divers have to be careful because corals have a thin layer of tissue over a hard skeleton of calcium carbonate. If a diver crashes into a coral, he or she could get cut badly.

"There are a lot of bacteria that live in association with the surface of the coral. You can get a really nasty infection." But, she says, "We do our best not to do that." And fortunately, it has never happened to her.

Richardson is quick to add that "there are a lot of nice things that happen down there, too." She recalls a time when she was doing a five-day study of the progression of black band disease that required her to be underwater for four or five hours a day. Near the reef she was studying lived some grouper fish that would peek around the corners of the coral and watch her. Some of them even followed her around. "It was amazing," she says. "To this day I won't eat grouper because of that experience."

Piecing a Puzzle Together

Richardson began her research on coral diseases around 1990. After more than 15 years, she says she is beginning to put together the pieces of the complex puzzle that makes up black band disease. It is complicated because it is a poly-microbial disease, which means it is caused by a whole bunch of different microbes working together.

"We haven't figured it out yet, but it has gotten to the point where it is like a jigsaw puzzle that is maybe seven-eighths of the way filled in. Anything we figure out now is one more piece of the puzzle, so that is really exciting."

What they have figured out so far is that as the disease-causing community of bacteria (dominated by blue-green algae) first grows, it quickly consumes the available oxygen. That opens the door for another group of bacteria, present in the ocean all the time, that thrive in an oxygen-free environment. Instead of oxygen, these bacteria use a compound called sulfate, which is dissolved in seawater, as a source of energy. They produce sulfide gas as a waste product.

"It turns out that sulfide gas is toxic to coral, and that starts killing the coral tissue. The dying coral tissue is then a source of nutrients and organic carbon for more bacteria. We also found out that the blue-green algae produce another toxin."

Unfortunately, she says, the main problem seems to be global warming. Global warming upsets the normal balance between corals and their environment.

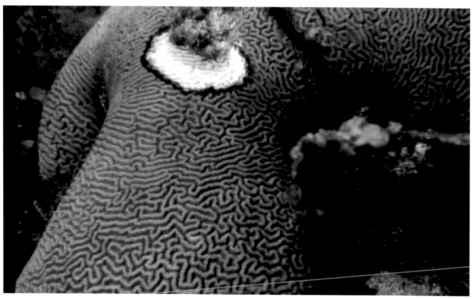

Dr. Richardson and her colleagues are starting to put together the pieces of the black band disease puzzle. They have discovered that the mysterious black bands are caused by bacteria releasing gas that is toxic to coral—probably due in part to global warming.

"We work on corals in tropical and subtropical reefs, and so they live in warm water, but when the water gets too warm they become stressed out. It's like us—if we are too cold our immune system doesn't really work that well." Corals don't really have an immune system, she says, but the problem is still similar.

Although the warmer water stresses the corals, microorganisms love it. When water temperatures go up, Richardson says, the growth of bacteria and blue-green algae "takes off like a rocket."

"In the meantime the corals they are living on become stressed and cannot defend themselves against infections, and what you get is disease."

Biologists may not be able to do anything about global warming, Richardson says, "but at least we can have some evidence that says this is a big part of the problem and people should really do something serious about global warming."

The work continues to be rewarding, Richardson says, for a couple of reasons. "We really do feel that we are figuring out what is going on with coral diseases."

Richardson's work may also shed light on human diseases. In fact, her current funding is from the National Institutes of Health. That is because many human diseases are also caused by a community of bacteria, not just a single germ. However, it is difficult to study those kinds of communities of bacteria in humans.

"You can't have humans being your lab rats," Richardson explains. However, she can take samples of the reef and try to better understand how many different microorganisms work together to cause disease.

Her work is also, Richardson notes, a wonderful teaching model. "I'm a biology professor, and my students are learning all about **ecology** [how organisms relate to their environment and other organisms] and physiology [how living organisms work] and microbiology and molecular **genetics** while they're out there in this incredible environment working on the reef."

So You Want to Be a Microbiologist?

For students who want to pursue a similar career, and maybe work in a similarly incredible environment, Richardson's advice is simple. "I always tell students the same thing: keep your grades up . . . keep your options open. Then when the time comes for you to make that decision and really pursue that career, you can be accepted into any program that you want to do," Richardson says.

This kind of work is very competitive, Richardson warns. "If you have not kept your grades up, and you go there and you apply . . . You'll get turned away right at the door."

And then, of course, you have to continue to keep your grades up all through college and graduate school, then try to get into a lab with somebody who is doing the kind of work you want to do.

That puts you in a position to take advantage of opportunities as they come along—just as Richardson did when she started working in remote sensing with NASA and ended up recognizing a microbial mat on a diseased reef in Florida during a dive just for fun.

How much the job pays depends on who is paying. If you are teaching at a university, you are paid a nine-month salary, and then are free to find research grants or do summer teaching over the remaining months. "Typically the nine-month salary for incoming professors at a pretty big university is about $65,000. The average for a full professor is about $90,000. But that is going to depend on the university. For a small university, or colleges, it is usually less than that."

Money Is Not Everything

Money is important, but it is not the most important thing, Richardson says. "It is really fun to be a scientist and make discoveries and figure out problems and make a story and piece together . . . what is going on with really complex interactions between species. That is really satisfying and rewarding."

As a friend of Richardson's likes to say, "Being a scientist is like being a kid all your life." A kid, in Richardson's case, who gets to spend her summers diving on coral reefs.

CHAPTER 5

Jonathan Runstadler: Investigating Avian Influenza

Every spring, an estimated six million birds arrive in Alaska to breed. They include waterfowl (such as geese and ducks) shorebirds (curlews and sandpipers), raptors (hawks and eagles) and landbirds (warblers, sparrows, and crows).[1]

Some of these birds spend the winter in South America, Central America, or southern North America. But some of them spend

Avian influenza virus

the winter in Southeast Asia, home to a strain of avian **influenza** (bird flu) called H5N1. Many scientists think this virus may eventually become a form of the flu that could kill millions of people worldwide in a global **pandemic**, an epidemic that spreads across a particularly large area.

It has happened before. An influenza pandemic in 1918 killed an estimated fifty million people, many of them healthy young adults. That set it apart from more common strains of influenza. Influenza kills thousands every year, but normally only those who are very elderly, very young, or already in a weakened condition due to other health problems.

Recently, scientists identified the virus that caused the 1918 pandemic as a strain of avian influenza. It jumped directly from birds to humans, and mutated, or changed, so it could be easily passed from person to person.

So far, H5N1 cannot be easily transmitted between people. Nevertheless, as of September 2008, there had been 387 confirmed cases of H5N1 in humans worldwide, and 245 deaths.[2]

The H5N1 virus has not yet shown up in North America. However, most scientists think it is only a matter of time. When it does arrive on this continent, a prime place for it to make its first appearance is Alaska. That is one reason Jonathan Runstadler, assistant professor of biology and wildlife at the University of Alaska Fairbanks Institute of Arctic Biology, and his associates have recently been spending a great deal of time swabbing the bottoms of birds.

Bird Flu Bonanza

The goal of their research is to learn more about how avian influenza viruses—of which there are more than 140 different types—circulate in Alaska's birds. They are also keeping an eye out for H5N1.

The project began in 2005. Many people besides Runstadler are involved. They take a swab of each bird's cloaca (the opening in a bird's rear end through which both urine and feces are expelled) and in some cases also obtain a swab from the bird's trachea, the breathing tube that carries air from the beak to the lungs. Sometimes they also collect samples of blood and feathers in order to examine the bird's genetic makeup.

Runstadler and his team are not capturing birds by themselves. Instead, they take advantage of some of the many other bird studies going on in Alaska at any given time.

Jonathan Runstadler spends much of his time in the field herding and swabbing birds. He tests the swab samples he collects for viruses—including avian influenza.

Runstadler and a colleague swab a bird's cloaca, the opening from which wastes are expelled.

"In Alaska, there is a lot of interest in bird work," Runstadler says. "A lot of people [go] up there to work on bird populations that breed and nest there and [raise] their young. What we have done is connect with those people and go out with them on field projects where they are getting their hands on birds."

Runstadler says there is a huge range of projects to choose from. He has worked with a researcher named Jim Sedinger, who studies Brant geese in the Yukon flats. Sedinger's team waits until the geese are molting (replacing old feathers with new ones) and are mostly unable to fly. Then they herd the geese down long, thin bits of land, bordered on either side by streams entering the Bering Sea, into temporary pens. "There can be anywhere from a hundred to a thousand geese at any one of these herdings," Runstadler says.

Sedinger's team members collect data on the birds' ages and molt status, and put metal bands on their legs so individual birds can be identified if they are captured another time. Runstadler and his colleagues collect their samples at the same time.

Another major site for Runstadler's team's work is in the Alaskan interior, not far from Fairbanks. There, with the Alaskan Department of Fish and Game, they band and capture birds, taking samples along the way.

A third major sampling site is within the city of Fairbanks itself, where the Alaska Bird Observatory does a lot of sampling of songbirds, which they capture using mist nets. A mist net is a fine-meshed net, similar to a volleyball net, that is invisible to the birds as they fly through the trees.

Digging for Droppings

In addition to collecting samples directly from birds, Runstadler's team samples the birds' environments.

"It's a big question mark as to what happens when the bird deposits the virus in the environment," Runstadler says.

It is thought that the virus stays in the bird population because infected birds leave waste in the environment. Other birds then pick up the virus by drinking contaminated water or mucking around in contaminated mud.

Runstadler's team samples mud and water in the summer and ice and frozen mud in the winter. They drill out ice cores and take mud samples from beneath the ice at the edges of frozen ponds, then look at those samples "both to detect virus and then see if we can grow virus from those samples."

The goal is to determine if environmental factors have an impact on the persistence of the virus and if the viruses can survive the winter and infect birds arriving in Alaska the following spring.

Interest in Animals Leads to Career

Runstadler grew up with a strong interest in animals and the environment. When he enrolled at Stanford University in California, it was natural for him to study biology.

IT ALL STARTED WITH WEASELS

Runstadler grew up in Hanover, New Hampshire, home to Dartmouth College and the Montshire Museum of Science, a hands-on science museum for kids. Runstadler took his first steps along the road to being a scientist in the fifth grade, when he did a school project on weasels. For that science project, students had to choose an animal and do a lot of research and writing about it.

"I chose the weasel—for what reason I can't exactly remember—and it so happened that the science education person who was in charge of the museum at the time was having an exhibit on weasels. I remember calling up and asking if I could meet with him and going over and talking with him about weasels.

"That's one of the things that I remember that influenced me, talking to somebody who was a scientist and who was interested in education. It was not just a book that I picked up and read about weasels. It was somebody that I talked to, and it was an exhibit that showed live weasels."

He even arranged to have a demonstration in his classroom of how the weasels were fed, but the school wouldn't allow it, fearing how kids (and likely their parents) might react to a weasel eating live mice in the classroom.

Runstadler remembers it all with humor: "My science project was censored!"

After he graduated, he worked for two different companies for a couple of years. One grew scallops in the Cape Cod area. The other was trying to develop an ecology-based method of processing wastewater (the water that goes down the drains in your house).

His experience with those companies boosted his interest in research, so he decided to go to graduate school. He intended to get a doctorate in molecular evolution, the study of the changes in DNA that drive evolution. However, just as he arrived at the University of New Hampshire in the early 1990s, the university launched a new program combining laboratory-based molecular science with environmental or ecology-based projects. That ended up being what he focused on.

That, in turn, got him interested in veterinary medicine. Runstadler ended up getting a dual PhD and Doctor of Veterinary Medicine degree from the University of California at Davis. After about ten years in Davis, he moved to Fairbanks.

"One of the reasons why I decided to accept the position in Fairbanks is Fairbanks has a strong history in studies in ecology, environmental science, and wildlife biology," Runstadler said. The university also had several research projects underway in which

CAMPING AND FLYING

Working in the field in Alaska means a lot of camping, Runstadler says, although some of the work done near Fairbanks can be completed on day trips. Larger bird samplings, especially waterfowl samplings, involve week-long or even two-week-long trips. For these samplings, Runstadler and his fellow researchers go out to field camps. "Sometimes those are pretty nice field camps. The Minto Flats area, where we do a lot of duck sampling, has a cabin that has a generator, and so people cook and so forth. Sometimes it's just tents and a regular camp site."

How do they get there? There is really only one way.

"In Alaska," Runstadler says, "you get everywhere by flying." Getting to the bigger sampling sites usually involves a trip in a float plane. "That's a lot of fun!"

involved in research projects like his usually discover they love it, he adds.

"There are a lot of things you can do as a kid your parents can help you with," he continues. "There are a lot of resources out there now for doing projects around your house or doing projects you find out about in the community that need volunteers. Maybe they need somebody to count birds during migration season—that can sometimes be done with just counting birds that come to your bird feeder during a certain time of year.

"There are more and more projects like that that are looking for a pool of volunteers to gather information. That is sometimes a lead-in to going further with projects or contacting other people."

Runstadler admits that spending part of your summer catching birds and taking swabs from their rear ends sounds strange. "I take a lot of grief for being somebody who looks at the bottom end of birds. But there are a lot of aspects of it that are enjoyable." That includes the fieldwork, he says, but also learning about the birds, "what they do, and what's special about them."

Runstadler says he has never had a scary moment, whether it be in direct contact with the birds or in his air travels throughout Alaska. But he does admit it is a bit scary thinking about the potential of picking up an infection from all the birds he handles.

Runstadler says that most experts in the field of influenza believe that at some point there will be a pandemic or very large outbreak that affects human populations. "Some have been convinced that it is going to happen with this H5N1 virus—some are convinced that it might be that one, but it might well be another one that we don't have our eye on as closely.

"The fact that there are viruses out there . . . that can potentially kill you is something that gives you second thoughts when you're out sampling those birds," he says, "but we take the precautions we feel are necessary, both in the fieldwork and in the lab work that we do."

But, Runstadler says, "that's really some of the motivation of it. Some of the work we do might lead to an understanding of these viruses that makes them less scary and dangerous on the whole."

That would be good news for all of us, even those of us who have never seen a bird's bottom.

CHAPTER 6

Jonathan Epstein: Bats and SARS

Teetering atop a twenty-foot-tall rocky spire in a cavern in China and trying to string a net to capture bats that may be carrying a deadly disease is all in a day's work for Jonathan Epstein.

Epstein is a veterinarian epidemiologist with the Consortium for Conservation Medicine. In 2004, he led the first expedition into China to try to determine if bats might

X-ray showing SARS infection

be the source of the virus that caused the deadly new illness known as Sudden Acute Respiratory Syndrome (SARS). Just two years before, SARS had sickened thousands and killed hundreds around the world.

Strange Pneumonia

The SARS outbreak began on November 16, 2002, when the first case of an unusual form of pneumonia was reported in Guangdong province in southern China. What made it unusual was that it was not caused by any of the usual germs that cause pneumonia. That meant that it also did not respond to the usual treatments.

As more cases of the strange illness began to crop up, the Chinese authorities tried to identify it—without success. But the world at large remained mostly unaware of the disease until, on February 28, 2003, the Vietnam French Hospital of Hanoi contacted the local office of the World Health Organization (WHO). The hospital wanted a doctor from WHO to come take a look at a patient with an unusual influenza-like illness.

Dr. Carlo Urbani responded to the call. He quickly realized that the hospital had a case of something unknown, dangerous—and worst of all, highly contagious. Before long, health workers in the hospital were also falling ill.

Dr. Urbani called the disease Sudden Acute Respiratory Syndrome.[1] By mid-March another outbreak of SARS had been reported in Hong Kong, and a patient in Toronto had died from the disease. WHO issued a global alert. There were fears of a global

Dr. Jonathan Epstein collected samples from various bat species to see how they are involved in the spread of deadly diseases such as SARS.

pandemic as SARS cropped up in more than two dozen countries in North America, South America, Europe, and Asia.

In the end, heroic efforts to identify and isolate those who had been exposed to the virus paid off. Within a few months, no more SARS cases were being reported anywhere. But over the course of the outbreak, 8,098 people had become ill, and 774 had died.[2]

Among those was Dr. Urbani. He contracted the disease at the hospital in Hanoi, and died on March 29, 2003, just a month after being called in to investigate.[3]

A New Strain of Virus

The global effort to identify the cause of SARS succeeded in a remarkably short time. On April 16, 2003, WHO announced that SARS was caused by a new strain of a type of virus called a coronavirus. Coronaviruses cause a variety of upper respiratory infections (including the common cold) in humans.

But where had this previously unknown strain come from?

Suspicion centered on the live animal markets of Guangdong, China, site of the first known human case. Most diseases that appear suddenly in humans are caused by viruses already circulating in animal populations that somehow make the leap from animals to humans.

WHO sent a team to Guangdong to test animals in the markets for the SARS coronavirus. The team tentatively concluded that the virus had jumped to humans from civets: small, catlike mammals native to the tropics of Africa and Asia. But although the strain of the virus they found in civets almost perfectly matched the virus isolated from the first human case, that did not necessarily mean civets were the natural reservoir, the animals the virus normally circulates among.

"As with any new disease, the tests are always less than perfect," Jonathan Epstein explains. "They had a bunch of spurious [false] positive results, not just civets, but a few other species—raccoons, dogs, some primate species—so there wasn't any sort of hard and fast evidence."

At the time, Epstein's research was focused on Nipah (pronounced NEE-pah) virus, which emerged in Malaysia and killed a hundred people by the end of June 1999. The virus first attacked the respiratory system in pigs, but then jumped to humans, causing encephalitis—brain inflammation. Several more outbreaks have occurred since the virus was first identified. Researchers found that the virus's natural reservoir was bats, and that the virus had jumped from them to pigs to humans.

Epstein was looking for research partners interested in testing bats in China for viruses related to Nipah virus. With that in mind, he talked to Hume Field, a veterinarian epidemiologist in Australia who was one of scientists involved in the first round of animal surveillance in the Guangdong marketplaces. Field wondered whether the SARS virus might also be circulating in Chinese bats.

Eventually there would be five separate expeditions to China to explore that question.

Off to China

Epstein led the first expedition. "There were bat biologists with expertise on a lot of things related to bats, but no one had a lot of experience collecting diagnostic samples from wild animals," he explains.

His main function was to lead the expedition in the wild and help catch the bats. He talked to the members of the expedition about how to protect themselves from infectious diseases. He also showed

Dr. Epstein and colleagues from China and Australia descend into a cave where they will look for bats that may be carrying the SARS coronavirus.

expedition members how to safely catch the bats without harming them and release them again after samples had been collected.

When people think of bats, they think of caves. But in fact, bats live in all kinds of different environments, from caves to attics to forests to (yes) belfries. It largely depends on their diet. Fruit-eating bats tend to live in the woods, while insect-eating bats tend to live in buildings or caves.

Most of the bats in China are insect-eaters, Epstein says. In the part of China where the expedition took place there were extensive cave systems, with some caverns as large as airplane hangars. "Some of the species of bats that we were looking at were also the ones that are traded in the market for food, particularly bats of the genus *Rhinolophus*," he says. "We were hiking into these cave systems, some of them about two kilometers long, looking for bat colonies we could catch."

To do so, they would string large "mist nets," similar to a volleyball net but with a much finer mesh, between two twenty-foot-tall bamboo poles.

Normally the poles are raised and anchored and the net strung between them along a flyway the bats might travel through. But within the caves, there wasn't a lot of solid ground in which to anchor the poles. As well, the ceilings were so high the bats could simply have flown over the top of the nets.

"We were actually climbing up stalagmites and perching on top of some of these rocky outcroppings that were twenty feet off the ground, two of us, each of us holding a pole and stringing these nets up between us," Epstein says. The goal was to get the net

A BIT ABOUT BATS

Bats are the only mammals that have evolved true flight: the ability to fly by flapping their wings, as opposed to simply gliding. There are more than 900 species worldwide, ranging in size from the huge Malayan flying fox, which can have a wingspan of more than five feet, to the Philippine bamboo bat, whose wingspan is only slightly over half an inch.

Various species eat small mammals, reptiles, birds, fish, other bats, fruit, flowers, nectar, pollen, leaves, and, in the case of the infamous vampire bat, blood.

close enough to the ceiling to catch the bats as they flew in.

In another case, the bats were roosting in a smaller cavern off of the main cave. The only way into the smaller cavern was through a tunnel high up in the wall of the main cave. To get the nets into the smaller cavern, "we fashioned ladders, and we climbed up to this hole that was probably about twelve feet in diameter [and] forty feet off the ground," Epstein says.

Still, Epstein thought it an improvement from other expeditions he had been on. While looking for Nipah virus in fruit bats living in mangrove swamps in Malaysia, he had to wade through five feet of water.

"Wherever you work with bats," Epstein says, "you

have to work at night, and you're dealing with wild animals that are much more adapted to their environment than [humans] are."

Harvesting Bats

A lot of the challenge in working with bats is setting the nets in the right places and making sure that you knows how the bats are going to fly, in which direction, and in what numbers. Assuming all the work has gone well, the bats end up unhurt but entangled in the mesh. Then you have to retrieve them without hurting them—or yourself.

Since the researchers believed that SARS could be transmitted by bats, they had to take precautions. Just inhaling dust from bat guano (feces) could have put the researchers at risk. To minimize that risk, the researchers wore long clothes, face masks with filters, safety glasses, and, of course, gloves made of a tough material that is puncture-resistant but allows for normal movement. Wearing gloves is always a good idea when handling bats, because bats "have pretty sharp teeth," Epstein notes.

As each bat was untangled, it was put into a small cloth bag in which the bats could hang. That calmed

In Malaysia, Epstein studied *Pteropus vampyrus*, which is the largest bat species in the world. This species is one of two that carry the deadly Nipah virus.

them. When the bats were calm, the scientists began collecting samples of blood, saliva, and feces.

"We would set up a mobile field lab, generally just a table where we had very small needles and syringes and sterile swabs," Epstein says. In addition to collecting samples, they would measure the bat's body length and forearm length.

The researchers did their best not to harm the animals—although, Epstein notes, there is always some stress to an animal when you are catching and manually restraining it. "That's where some of my expertise as a veterinarian came in," he says, "being able to restrain wild animals without hurting them or without getting hurt."

Eureka!

The samples were then taken back to the lab to be tested for SARS coronavirus, and . . . eureka! The scientists discovered that between 30 and 40 percent

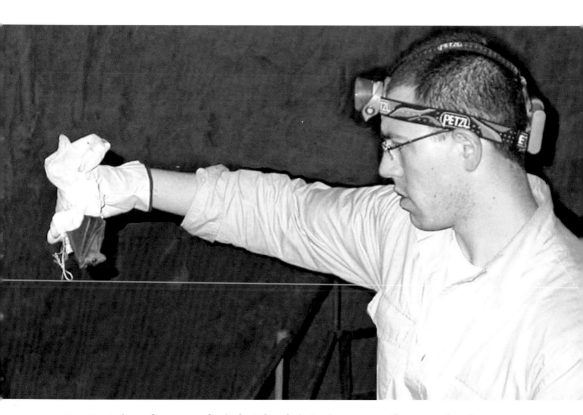

Dr. Epstein releases a fruit bat back into its cave. The samples he collected from this and other species were tested for SARS coronavirus.

of the bats from the *Rhinolophus* genus tested positive for **antibodies** for SARS coronavirus, even though they were not sick and (obviously) not dead. "That suggests that the virus has spread through a good proportion of the population, and that those animals have survived infection with antibodies and are now resistant," Epstein explains.

Laboratories in China and Australia were also able to detect some of the virus's genetic material in the samples from the bats. The presence of antibodies proved that the bats had been exposed to the virus. The presence of genetic material proved that they were still carrying it.

The lab results revealed four or five different viruses within the bats, all within the SARS coronavirus family. "When you look at a family tree of these viruses, the virus that infected humans in the outbreak in 2002–2003 fit right inside," Epstein says. Dubbing the human viruses "SARS-like coronaviruses," the researchers realized they were close to solving the puzzle and that a lot of what was happening was due to bats being caught from the wild and brought into Guangdong and other similar marketplaces.

The Marketplace Menagerie

Those marketplaces, Epstein explained, are "a complete menagerie [zoo]. There are animals of all species, of all types, alive and dead, being kept together in very unhygienic [dirty] conditions. As soon as someone picks one out, they butcher it with bare hands right there on site, so there is plenty of opportunity for cross-infection to occur among different animals."

Putting all the pieces together, scientists now presume that bats infected with a SARS-like coronavirus were brought into the marketplace, where they came in contact with civets. In the civets, the virus mutated. It then jumped from civets to people, which is why the virus found in civets was so similar to the one found in people.

Why did it happen now, when bats have presumably been carrying the virus—and have been brought into the Chinese marketplaces—for a long time?

"A lot of it has to do with just luck and probability," Epstein says. "Bats have been brought in for a long time. Some have been infected, some have not. The ones that are infected have to be able to infect other animals, and the virus has to change such that it can readily infect both another species and then people."

Understanding the process is important, Epstein says, because scientists fear that what happened with SARS could happen with avian influenza (bird flu). The virus's goal is to spread, and, with the right combination, it could one day be easily transmitted from person to person. For a virus, says Epstein, "It's no good if it just gets somebody sick and then they recover without transmitting it."

Why Not Wipe Out the Bats?

Part of the mission of Epstein's employer, the Consortium for Conservation Medicine, is to point out that problems such as the emergence of the SARS virus arise from human behavior, not from anything the animals have done.

Human activities that create opportunities for diseases in animals to spill over into people are called "anthropogenic factors" by researchers. "Normally people and animals wouldn't interact if it weren't for these activities," Epstein explains.

Anthropogenic factors include trade in wildlife (such as that within the Chinese markets), global travel, and industrialization or agricultural expansion. Expansion of farms into wildlife habitats, like a rain forest, increases the interaction between wild animals and humans and domestic animals (pets and livestock) more than ever before. This is why we are seeing more emerging diseases than we have previously, says Epstein.

But, Epstein says, "the knee-jerk reaction from the public may be 'Well, if these bats are carrying a disease that kills people, why not just get rid of the bats?' Our job is to say, 'No, these animals serve a very important function ecologically.'"

Epstein points out that insect-eating bats are important for pest control and fruit-eating bats are vital to many plants as pollinators and seed-dispersers. "You can't just eliminate them. One, you would lose those ecological services. Two, if you remove them from an ecosystem you never know what might move in to take their place. You create a vacuum, and something worse could come in that carries even worse diseases."

To deal with emerging diseases, Epstein says, we need to better understand how people and animals interact, not simply try to eliminate the animals carrying the diseases. "We need to recognize that human activities are what are causing these diseases to emerge. It's not the fault of the animals," he says.

Human and Animal Health Are Connected

Studying the interaction of humans and animals comes naturally to Epstein. When he went to veterinary school he already knew he wanted to work with wildlife. He also had a strong interest in the conservation of wild species.

The school he attended, Tufts University in Massachusetts, had a fairly new program at the time which combined a doctorate in veterinary medicine with a master's degree in public health. Over the four years of his veterinary training, Epstein also took classes at the medical school with medical students interested in focusing on public health.

"In the course of [my study] I started to see that there was a very real connection between human health and animal health," Epstein says. "That particularly was apparent with infectious diseases, because there are so many diseases out there that came from animals . . . also, a lot of the emerging diseases we see come from animals."

Becoming a veterinarian epidemiologist was a way to work with wildlife and focus on improving human health at the same time, a combination that appealed to Epstein.

"Veterinarians have worked in public health for a while, but in the past ten years there has been a real recognition that human health issues and animal health issues are linked," Epstein says. "What has been really fascinating is that traditional barriers between physicians who work in public health, veterinarians, and other scientists—including virologists and ecologists—are melting away. You see a lot more collaborative teams that include people from a whole lot of different disciplines."

It is work, he says, that he finds "very exciting" and "incredibly rewarding" . . . even when he is wading five feet deep in mangrove swamps in Malaysia or scaling slimy stalagmites in Chinese caves.

Ebola in Uganda

In the movie *Outbreak*, a kind of super-Ebola virus—which kills everyone who contracts it—arrives in the United States, carried by an infected African monkey. Researchers from the U.S. Army Medical Research Institute for Infectious Diseases and the Centers for

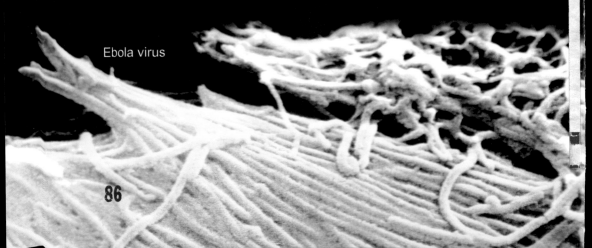

Ebola virus

Disease Control and Prevention (CDC) have to figure out how to stop it. *Outbreak* came out in 1995—the same year that Marta Guerra was finishing her master's degree in public health.

Guerra had grown up in Washington, D.C., exposed to a lot of different cultures. In high school she decided to become a veterinarian. She received her Doctor of Veterinary Medicine degree from the University of Florida in 1985. While practicing as a vet, she says, she became very interested in zoonotic diseases—diseases that come from animals—and science education. "At some point I decided I would go back to school and do public health."

And then she went to see *Outbreak*. "I was looking around for work, and I remember seeing that movie and thinking, 'Wow, that's what I want to do!'"

Fast-forward to November 2000. Guerra, now with a PhD in epidemiology and recently hired as an officer of the Epidemic Intelligence Service (EIS) program of the CDC, received orders to head out on her first international mission. She would be helping to study and combat an outbreak in Uganda, Africa, of Ebola virus—the very virus the disease in *Outbreak* was based upon. "It was very ironic," she says.

It was also unexpected. "I had done a couple of

Marta Guerra's work in epidemiology sometimes takes her to faraway places. This photo was taken after she visited a health clinic in Ethiopia.

days of a domestic [in the U.S.] case investigation but I really did not expect to be asked to go on an international trip that early. Basically I heard rumors on a Tuesday and by Thursday we heard we were going—and leaving Sunday."

Quick Departure

The next couple of days were a whirlwind of preparation. That Friday, she headed to the health clinic to get all of the necessary vaccinations. "I think I received about five shots in one day to prepare," Guerra recalls. Arrangements also had to be made for her to travel on her personal passport, because she did not have an official passport—a special passport issued to employees of the United States assigned overseas.

"Our embassy has to agree that you can come to the country, so there is a lot of paperwork involved." And then there was all the equipment to assemble. She wanted to make sure she had plenty of personal protection equipment: gloves, booties, and masks.

Guerra flew to Africa with another, more experienced EIS officer, and two laboratory technicians. They joined five other team members from the CDC who were already in Lacor, Uganda, working in a laboratory set up at St. Mary's Hospital, a private hospital established by an Italian doctor. St. Mary's had much more advanced equipment than the local government-run hospital. It was already set up with the equipment Dr. Guerra and her colleagues needed, so the team was able to diagnose people in less than 24 hours.

Accurate diagnosis was important, she says, not only to identify people who had Ebola, but to identify those who did not so that they could keep healthy people separate from the suspected Ebola patients.

Tracking the Disease

Guerra's work during the outbreak included tracking the spread of the disease, identifying those who had been exposed, and educating the public.

WHAT IS EBOLA?

Ebola fever is a deadly disease that gets its name from the Ebola River near Yambuku, Democratic Republic of the Congo, Africa. That region was the site of the first recognized outbreak.

Ebola begins with influenza-like symptoms: fever, weakness, muscle pain, headache and sore throat. Eventually, vomiting, diarrhea, and rash develop. The kidneys and liver may stop functioning normally. In fatal cases, uncontrollable internal and external bleeding begins, resulting in the vomiting of blood, and bleeding from the eyes, ears, nose, and other body openings.

The disease is transmitted through direct contact with the blood or other bodily fluids (sweat, saliva, etc.) of the infected person or by contact with objects contaminated with infected bodily fluids. No airborne transmission of Ebola has ever been documented in humans.

Currently, there is no effective treatment for Ebola. The best doctors can do is treat the symptoms until the patient's own immune system can fight off the infection on its own—if it is able to. Treatment includes intravenous fluids and oxygen; drugs to control fever, help the blood clot, and maintain blood pressure; and antibiotics to prevent secondary infections from bacteria.

"Part of what we did was to try to organize the database, to make sure that we had everyone who was in the hospital listed, and that we had all of the contacts listed," she says. Every day Guerra and other doctors and volunteers would go to the government-run hospital and get the list of people who were newly admitted and newly diagnosed. "Then we would go out to the person's home and make a list of [his or her] contacts. Those contacts would have to be visited for 21 days. If there was anyone that appeared to be unhealthy or developing any kind of symptoms, then we would call . . . the hospital to bring an ambulance out," Guerra said.

In total, about 150 trained volunteers helped in this surveillance project. Over the course of the outbreak, 5,600 people who had been in contact with infected patients were identified and observed.

Another important component of Guerra's work was education, a process helped by the fact that, in Uganda, most of the people who have attended school understand English. Guerra and her team would visit villages—some just small groups of huts placed close together—and announce the reason for their visit and what was happening. Guerra found that the locals "had amazing questions. Without

This photo was taken outside the hospital where Guerra helped review the medical records of Ebola patients.

having medical knowledge they were asking a lot of good questions as far as transmission and how to protect themselves."

Unlearning the Lessons of HIV

The Ugandan government, Guerra says, had done a wonderful job educating people about another deadly virus that plagues the region: **HIV**, the virus that causes AIDS. But the lessons learned regarding HIV actually made it harder to deal with Ebola.

"HIV is very different," Guerra points out. "Once you are positive you stay positive, and most likely you are eventually going to die from it. So they transferred that concept into, 'OK, your test was positive for Ebola, therefore you're positive for Ebola and you're going to have it for the rest of your life.'"

She says it took a lot of work to get the people to understand the difference between HIV and Ebola. When you test positive for antibodies to HIV, it means you're infected with a disease that will most likely kill you and can be passed on to other people. But, if you survive Ebola, you are no longer contagious and the antibodies in your body protect you from contracting the disease again. "It was sort of trying to tease out some very specific scientific concepts about immunology and then trying to explain it to them in terms they understood."

Because of what they'd learned about HIV, Guerra says, people thought that anyone with antibodies to Ebola was contagious and was dangerous to have around. As a result, survivors of the disease were being cast out from the villages, away from their families, with no food, because people feared sharing their food with Ebola survivors or letting them use their dishes.

It became an important part of the education process for Guerra to show others that touching and interacting with these survivors was not dangerous.

"I would definitely go up and touch them, or try to show them that I was not scared to be around them." She would often give the survivors money so they could buy food or pots and pans and something to sleep on.

Another aspect of education was telling local residents that they had to go immediately to the hospital to get checked out if they experienced any flu-like symptoms. That was important, Guerra says, because it meant that those who were infected did not have time to transmit the virus to anyone else.

Most people in the area would first be cared for by family members when they became ill, Guerra explains. After that, they would probably turn to traditional healers. "They wouldn't necessarily go to a clinic, because there are usually very few of them and it would be a very far walk," Guerra says. That led to tragedies like the death of all four sisters in one family because they took care of each other as they fell ill one by one.

To avoid that, the team members urged the local people to go to a clinic as soon as they felt ill. "If it was malaria, then good, you got your treatment early and you'd be on your way to recovery," she would tell them. On the other hand, if it was Ebola, victims could quickly be isolated from their family, and supportive care could be started.

Only Concerned Once

Despite the well-publicized deadliness of Ebola, Guerra says she was not particularly concerned about the risk of contracting the disease herself. "Because I was going as an epidemiologist, I didn't think I was going to be actually taking care of patients," she says. "My role was working with the local health department and all of the other international organizations that were there. Because I knew how to protect myself as far as wearing all the personal protection equipment, I wasn't nervous at that time."

But she did get concerned about being exposed on one visit to the home of an Ebola patient who had a little boy who was about two years old. "She was in the hospital at the time, and we were out checking her family. The little boy at first was very scared of me, but after three or four days he finally came up to me and gave me this big hug around my legs, and I hugged him back. The next day we came out and the little boy was not there, and they said they had to take him to the hospital.

"[I was] thinking, 'Well, could it be Ebola?' Here I was in very close contact with him the day before."

Fortunately, for both Guerra and the little boy, his symptoms were due to malaria, not Ebola.

The researchers were more worried about people than viruses, Guerra recalls. "We were in the territory of the Lord's Resistance Army [a rebel group] in northern Uganda. A lot of people had been displaced up there, a lot of people kidnapped and killed, so there was a curfew. Every day we had to try to make sure we got home before dark. When you are in these kinds of conditions you are working around the clock. It was very difficult to pack everything up and go home."

Guerra's scariest moments came one night when the team missed the curfew and had to drive home in the dark. "There are woods on either side. It's at night, and there is no streetlight. It's a dirt road, and unless there is a moon out, it is just pitch black. The headlights only go maybe ten or fifteen feet ahead of the car. By the time you see somebody they are quite close.

"It's just amazing how many people are traveling the roads, just walking, at night. A couple of times, you would come up, you would see some people in uniforms, and it was hard to tell whether they were soldiers from the Ugandan army or whether they could possibly be some of these rebels."

There was reason to be concerned: some scientists from South Africa were shot at by snipers during one trip into the war-torn north.

The hospital and the center of Lacor were considered safe, Guerra says, and most of the Ebola patients her team visited were close to the town, within about five kilometers. However, when they heard of a case further north in one of the refugee camps, they needed a military escort to check it out.

"It was a very different atmosphere in the refugee camp. Everyone was very quiet and very suspicious. People were starting rumors that we wanted to take their blood in order to sell it, so we were not getting very much cooperation as far as drawing samples. Everybody just seemed very tense and very scared."

In the end, though, Guerra's team saw nothing of the Lord's Resistance Army. "I think they were also very scared of the Ebola outbreak," she says.

They had good reason to be frightened. The 2000 Ugandan outbreak killed 225 people before it was brought under control.

"A Wonderful Experience"

Guerra remained in Uganda for a month. Despite the deadliness of the disease and the danger from the rebels, she calls the experience "just wonderful."

"For people who like to do fairly exciting things, not just for the thrill of it but also to feel like you are actually helping people, it was a wonderful experience," she says.

There were scientific benefits as well. "Whenever these things happen, it is always a chance to learn more about the disease and how it spreads, so that hopefully the next time it comes up you can apply your preventive measures a little bit faster and better."

The Uganda outbreak was different from previous outbreaks of Ebola because of the fairly sophisticated laboratory equipment available to the doctors and researchers. Doctors had found that many of the people who seemed to recover (about half, in the Ugandan outbreak) were not recovering well. "They were not feeling like they were getting their energy back," Guerra says.

Thanks to the equipment available at St. Mary's Hospital, the CDC team was able to do some of the laboratory tests that are usually done in other hospitals around the world to diagnose problems.

What they found was the recovering patients had very low levels of the mineral potassium. Providing the patients with extra potassium was an easy and effective solution. "They almost looked like they came back to life, and they were able to recover and go home much more quickly. That was something that we did not know beforehand. You always figure if you go through the acute phases of the disease and you survive you should be bouncing back quickly. It was interesting finding out that there are maybe other reasons why people are not."

More People Always Needed

There is always a need for more people to work in the field of epidemiology, in outbreaks like the one in Uganda, Guerra says. Even though a lot of people think the work sounds very exciting, there are not many people who would actually be willing to go. "A lot of times you have difficulty recruiting people to go to work in these kinds of conditions," Guerra says.

She recommends that young people considering a career in epidemiology work toward some kind of health-professional degree. "It doesn't necessarily have to be medical," she says. "It could be dental, it could be veterinary, it could be a master's in public

More people are always needed to help in the field of epidemiology, like these social workers who taught children about how to avoid the Ebola virus during the 2000 outbreak in Uganda.

health or a PhD in epidemiology or some kind of laboratory science."

The important thing, she says, is to focus on dealing with populations—groups of people with something in common—as opposed to individuals. "You still have to learn the medicine at the individual level, but definitely look at diseases that are communicable [contagious] and try to focus on types of professions that deal with people in larger populations."

Of course getting good grades in science and math classes is important, Guerra says, "but we always seem to forget that you need good communication skills. I still recommend doing well in English and being able to write well and having experience in communicating with others."

Education is important. But it might also be worthwhile to rent the movie *Outbreak*, Guerra says. Of course it's not an entirely accurate portrayal of life as a disease detective, but "the value in those films is opening up the idea that there could be diseases out there that we still don't know—there's still so much about science that we don't know." And, she adds, there are "chances to go out there and help people who are in a very disadvantaged state…chances to go out there and do investigations."

From high-tech laboratories to some of the most disadvantaged parts of the world, from busy cities to distant jungles, from Chinese caves to coral reefs, the career of a disease detective may take him or her to some surprising, exciting, and even dangerous places.

But as you can see, the work is seldom boring. As the world continues to change and more diseases emerge from the shadows, it is work that is going to become more and more important—to us, and to all the other species we share this planet with.

Appendix: Careers in Epidemiology

Scientist	Title	Education	Average Salary
Lisa Fernando	Biologist, Special Pathogens, National Microbiology Laboratory, Canadian Science Centre for Human and Animal Health	Bachelor of science degree in biology; master's degree in medical microbiology	$38,000 to $80,000
James Strong	Medical Officer, Head of Cell Biology Division, Special Pathogens, National Microbiology Laboratory, Canadian Science Centre for Human and Animal Health	Bachelor of science degrees in zoology and cellular, molecular and microbial biology; PhD in molecular virology; MD (medical doctor degree)	$60,000 to $105,000
Laurie Richardson	Professor of Biology, Florida International University	Bachelor of arts degree in fine arts, chemistry, and environmental biology; PhD in microbiology	$65,000 to $90,000
Jonathan Runstadler	Assistant Professor of Biology and Wildlife, University of Alaska Fairbanks Institute of Arctic Biology	Bachelor of science degree in biology; master's degree in zoology; PhD in genetics; DVM (doctor of veterinary medicine degree)	$70,000 to $90,000
Jonathan Epstein	Senior Research Scientist, Consortium for Conservation Medicine	Master's degree in public health; DVM (doctor of veterinary medicine degree); certificate in international veterinary medicine	$45,220 to $71,080
Marta Guerra	Physicist, Postdoctoral Research Fellow, Officer: Epidemic Intelligence Service (EIS), Centers for Disease Control and Prevention	Master's degree in public health; PhD in epidemiology; DVM (doctor of veterinary medicine degree)	$40,000 to $60,000 with a master's degree, $120,000 to $130,000 with an MD or PhD

Chapter Notes

Chapter 1. Chasing Disease

1. L.H. Taylor, S.M. Latham, and M.E. Woolhouse, "Risk factors for human disease emergence," *Philosophical transactions of the Royal Society of London, Series B, Biological sciences*, Vol. 356, No. 1411 (29 July 2001), pp. 983–989, <http://www.citeulike.org/user/skumagai/article/2876956> (June 23, 2008).

Chapter 2. Lisa Fernando: Marburg in Angola

Telephone interview with Lisa Fernando, September 26, 2007. All quotes from Fernando come from this interview.

Chapter 3. James Strong: Working In Level 4

Telephone interview with Dr. James Strong, September 24, 2007. All quotes from Strong come from this interview.

1. Centers for Disease Control and Prevention, "Biosafety," n.d. <http://www.cdc.gov/od/ohs/pdffiles/Module%202%20-%20Biosafety.pdf> (June 26, 2008).
2. Kelly Keith, Canadian Science Centre for Human and Animal Health, e-mail message to author, September 20, 2007.

Chapter 4. Laurie Richardson:
What's Killing the Coral?

Telephone interview with Dr. Laurie Richardson, September 12, 2007. All quotes from Richardson come from this interview.

1. Ian James, "Fragile Coral Reefs Are Dying," Cyber Diver News Network, n.d. <http://www.cdnn.info/news/article/a011223.html> (February 29, 2008).

Chapter 5. Jonathan Runstadler:
Investigating Avian Influenza

Telephone interview with Jon Runstadler, September 28, 2007. All quotes from Runstadler come from this interview.

1. U.S. Fish and Wildlife Service, "Migratory Bird Management," September 15, 2008, <http://alaska.fws.gov/mbsp/mbm/index.htm> (June 30, 2008).
2. World Health Organization, "Avian Influenza," n.d., <http://www.who.int/csr/disease/avian_influenza/en/index.html> (June 30, 2008).

Chapter 6. Jonathan Epstein: Bats and SARS

Telephone interview with Jonathan Epstein, September 14, 2007. All quotes from Epstein come from this interview.

1. Brigg Reilley, Michel Van Herp, Dan Sermand, and Nicoletta Dentico, "SARS and Carlo Urbani," New England Journal of Medicine, May 15, 2003. <http://content.nejm.org/cgi/content/full/348/20/1951> (February 29, 2008).
2. Centers for Disease Control and Prevention, "Frequently Asked Questions About SARS," May 3, 2005, <http://www.cdc.gov/NCIDOD/SARS/faq.htm> (February 29, 2008).
3. Reilley et al.

Chapter 7. Marta Guerra: Ebola in Uganda

Telephone interview with Marta Guerra, October 10, 2007. All quotes from Guerra come from this interview.

1. MedTV, "Ebola Treatment," n.d., <http://ebola.emedtv.com/ebola/ebola-treatment.html> (December 9, 2008).

Glossary

algae—Microscopic plants or plantlike organisms.

antibodies—Substances produced by the body to fight off specific infections.

bacteria—Single-celled microscopic organisms, some of which can cause disease.

biosafety—The steps taken in a laboratory to protect researchers and the public from disease-causing agents.

ecology—The study of how living things interact with each other and their environment.

emerging disease—A disease that has just appeared or has suddenly become more widespread.

epidemiology—The study of how often diseases affect different groups of people or animals, and why.

genetics—The study of how traits are passed down from generation to generation.

HIV—Human Immunodeficiency Virus, the virus that causes AIDS.

influenza—A severe respiratory disease, caused by a virus. Commonly called "the flu."

isolation ward—A hospital room with special features designed to prevent the spread of infectious diseases from patients kept inside it.

malaria—A mosquito-transmitted disease caused by microscopic parasites that infect the red blood cells.

microbial—Related to microscopic organisms.

microbiology—The study of microscopic organisms.

pandemic—A disease that occurs globally over a wide area and affects a high percentage of people or animals.

pathogen—Something (usually a virus or bacterium) that causes disease.

reservoir species—An animal species that can carry a pathogen without suffering from the disease.

virology—The study of viruses.

virus—Extremely tiny disease-causing agents that can only reproduce by infecting living cells.

zoonotic—A disease transmitted from animals to humans.

Further Reading

Friedlander, Mark P., Jr. *Outbreak: Disease Detectives at Work*. Minneapolis: Lerner Publishing Group, 2002.

Grady, Denise. *Deadly Invaders: Virus Outbreaks Around the World, From Marburg Fever to Avian Flu*. Boston: Kingfisher, 2006.

Serradell, Joaquima. *SARS (Deadly Diseases and Epidemics)*. New York: Chelsea House, 2005.

Internet Addresses

KidsHealth. "Bird Flu (Avian Flu)."
<http://kidshealth.org/kid/health_problems/infection/
bird_flu.html>

National Institute of Environmental Health Sciences.
"NIEHS Kids' Pages."
<http://kids.niehs.nih.gov/home.htm>

Science News for Kids. "Disease Detectives."
<http://www.sciencenewsforkids.org/articles/20061115/
Feature1.asp>

Index